West Africa's Political Econ
Millennium: Retrospect and Prospect

Adebayo Olukoshi

Monograph Series 2/2001

West Africa's Political Economy in the Next Millennium: Retrospect and Prospect

Council for the Development of Social Science Research in Africa
Avenue Cheikh Anta Diop Angle Canal IV, BP: 3304, Dakar, Senegal

OXFAM GB/I
274 Banbury Road, Oxford, 0X2 7DZ, United Kingdom

Typeset by Hadijatou Sy
Printed by CODESRIA

CODESRIA Monograph Series
ISBN 2-86978-104-0

CODESRIA would like to express its gratitude to the Swedish Development Co-operation Agency (SIDA/SAREC), the International Development Research Centre (IDRC), OXFAM GB/I, the Mac Arthur Foundation, the Carnegie Corporation, the Norwegian Ministry of Foreign Affairs, the Danish Agency for International Development (DANIDA), the French Ministry of Cooperation, the Ford Foundation, the United Nations Development Programme (UNDP), the Rockefeller Foundation, the Prince Claus Fund and the Government of Senegal for support of its research, publication and training activities.

Contents

Author

Adebayo Olukoshi is Professor of International Relations and graduated from Ahmadu Bello University, Zaria and Leeds University, England. He was Director of Research at the Nigerian Institute of International Affairs, Lagos and Programme Officer at the Nordiska Afrikainstitutet, Uppsala. He is currently Executive Secretary of the Council for the Development of Social Science Research in Africa (CODESRIA), Dakar. He has published extensively on contemporary politics in Africa.

Introduction

The West African sub-region is unique in many important respects. Home to the world's most populous black country (Nigeria) and Africa's oldest republic (Liberia), it is also the region which produced the first African country (Ghana in 1957) to win its independence from European colonial rule. Ghana's example of radical nationalist agitation served as a source of inspiration for Sékou Touré who, in mobilising opposition to Charles de Gaulle's offer of independence within the French Community, ushered Guinea-Conakry into independence as the first Francophone African country to jettison colonial rule. Guinea-Conakry's defiance was to rapidly pave the way for the formal independence of the rest of the countries of Francophone Africa. Additionally, it is in West Africa that one of the first military coups d'état in post-independence Africa took place when members of the Togolese armed forces toppled and murdered Sylvanus Olympio. Since the Togolese coup d'etat of January 1963, West Africa has developed a reputation as the coup d'état belt of the African continent, with only two of the countries in the sub-region, Senegal and Côte d'Ivoire, having managed to escape direct military rule until the latter was eventually overcome by its crises, succumbing to the military coup at the turn of the twentieth century in December 1999. All the other fourteen West African countries have each experienced an average of about three coups d'état since the early 1960s; the number of attempted coups is countless.

Prolonged military rule in West Africa has not only generated deep-seated political instability, it has also fanned a growing culture of militarism which has combined with other factors, not least among them deep-seated economic decline and widespread youth disaffection, to propel several countries in the sub-region into full-scale war. Thus, Liberia was led into a lengthy and ruinous war following the outbreak of an armed rebellion against the military dictatorship of Samuel Doe; Sierra Leone was soon to follow as a section of the armed forces joined rebels of the Revolutionary United Front (RUF) to plunder the country and wreak havoc on the populace. Guinea-Bissau too was to slide into a civil war in 1998 that culminated in the overthrow of Joào Nino Vieira from power in May 1999. In Niger and Mali, two Francophone countries that have been exposed to some of the harshest forms of military authoritarianism, repeated armed clashes occurred during the late 1980s and in the 1990s between the army and Touareg rebels fighting for greater autonomy. Countries such as Nigeria (which had a civil war from 1967 to 1970), Guinea-Conakry, and Ghana have on occasions tottered on the brink of outright war and the breakdown of civil order. The two countries that

1

have not had a history of direct military rule have also had their share of authoritarian, even personal rule.

Yet, in spite of the experience of prolonged military rule, the West African sub-region has a thriving civil society and was in the forefront of the movement, in the late 1980s and early 1990s, towards political liberalisation. Indeed, the innovative and popular sovereign national conferences that were held in several Francophone and Lusophone African countries were first convened in West Africa, beginning with Bénin Republic. Associational life also has a long history in West Africa and although the worst authoritarian regimes did attempt to stifle the development of the different civic associations, especially those organised by students and various urban-based interest groups, it has proved difficult to completely undermine them. These associations were in the vanguard of the resistance to continued colonial domination and the growth of post-colonial authoritarian rule; they were also to play a leading role in the quest for political reforms that was witnessed in the late 1980s and early 1990s. The long history of civil society activism in West Africa was underpinned by the lively intellectual and political environments associated with the *Négritude* of Sedar Senghor, the *Egyptology* of Cheikh Anta Diop, and the radical *Pan-Africanism* of Kwame Nkrumah. So strong were these politico- intellectual strands that West Africa, during the post-1945 period up to the mid-1970s, became, at one time or the other, a credible base for a variety of black philosophers and activists, ranging from long-term residents like George Padmore and Frantz Fanon to short-term visitors like C.L.R. James and Abdurahman Babu.

Unlike the other regions of Africa, West Africa did not experience settler forms of colonialism — certainly, no where in West Africa were the kinds of spirited attempts at developing white settler colonialism as occurred in such places as South Africa, Namibia, Zimbabwe, Mozambique, Kenya, Algeria, and the Belgian Congo (Zaire) ever experienced. The general explanation for the absence of settler colonial rule in West Africa centres on the prevalence of malaria in the mosquito-infested rain forest and savannah belts of the region. The deadly toll in lives which the West African mosquito exacted on the early European explorers, missionaries, and colonial officials was a key factor which dissuaded white settler colonial rule in the sub-region. It is, however, also possible that the widespread influence of Islam in the savannah belts of the area also played a part, especially as a number of the pre-colonial political formations in the area, not least the Sokoto Caliphate, the Kanem Bornu Empire, the Bambara states, and the various Senegambian states, were already built along theocratic lines. Partly on account of the absence of settler colonialism in the area, the struggles for independence in West Africa, though intense and vigorous, did not, in most cases, result in the kinds of sustained and prolonged armed struggles that characterised the experiences of most of the settler colonies of East, Southern, and North Africa. Only in the Portuguese colonies of Guinea Bissau and Cape Verde were armed struggles fought to force independence on the colonising power, a fact that was reflective, in part at least, of the backwardness of Portugal as a colonial power.

That armed liberation wars were not fought to usher most of the countries of West Africa into independence was, taken in a historical context, ironical. For it was in West Africa that some of the stiffest wars of resistance to colonial rule were encountered by the forces of European imperialism. Prior to the arrival of the forces of colonialism, the West African sub-region was dotted by a host of kingdoms and empires among the Ashanti Kingdom to the Sokoto Caliphate, the Kanem Bornu, Samory Touré's Guinea, the Oyo, the Benin and the Dahomey Kingdom, among others. Some of these established political structures were to form the focal point of the armed resistance to colonial incursion in West Africa. The pre-colonial political formations represented some of the most advanced efforts at nation-state building in Africa; not surprisingly, a host of vested interests had developed around them to make resistance to the colonial incursion almost inevitable. Once the armed resistance to the colonial incursion was defeated, the colonial powers proceeded to introduce measures aimed at facilitating their rule. In the Francophone and, to a lesser extent, Lusophone colonies, the main mode of control that was developed centred around the policy of assimilation and the goal of obliterating local cultures and creating black French/Portuguese men and women; in Anglophone Africa, 'indirect rule' which entailed reliance on existing, if re-oriented, 'traditional' structures of governance tended to be the norm. Irrespective of the mode of colonial governance that emerged, West Africa was to become the sub-region of Africa where the earliest intellectual and political currents against colonial rule developed most fully; in many cases, these currents fed into a wider pan-Africanist agenda aimed at recapturing the history and identity of the entire black race. Not surprisingly, it was also in West Africa, specifically in Accra, that the first Pan-African congress to be held on African soil took place, attracting the participation of the key nationalist and intellectual leaders of Africa and the diaspora.

This study proposes to examine various trends and structural factors in the contemporary political economy of West Africa with a view to assessing how they are likely to affect the needs and capabilities of the countries of the sub-region in the next millennium. This assessment is carried out not only in the context of the demands within the sub-region for achieving a more rapid system of democratic development, but also in relation to the ways in which West Africa might more fully respond to the demands of globalisation. In undertaking the study, particular attention is paid to the following issues: population, food security, poverty, democracy, human rights, civil society and governance, macro-economic developments, the external debt problems of the countries, the prospects for regional co-operation/integration, the extremely important geo-political and economic role which France plays in West Africa, and the changing forms of popular identity, with emphasis on Islam and its growing relative influence. The study is presented in an overview form and in a manner that is intended to be both retrospective and prospective. It is argued that in this age of intensifying globalisation, West Africa's future centres around a choice between closer regional co-operation and the continued pursuit of individual national strategies which are often not co-ordinated on a regional basis. The difficult question is whether the necessary political will can be found to make the choice that will help unlock the full potentials of the countries of the sub-region.

The West African Sub-Region: A Panorama of Main Trends and Structural Factors

The Demographic Picture

West Africa consists of a total of 16 states, excluding Cameroon which is usu-ally categorised as belonging to Central Africa. It is, by far, one of Africa's most populous regions. With a population of about 245 million people in 1998, it accounts for almost two out of every four Africans living on the conti-nent. In the period between 1960 and 1995, the population of the sub-region increased by a staggering total of 130 million people. At an average growth rate of 3% per annum, it is forecast that the sub-region will have a population of about 430 million in 2020, a trend which is not expected to be too adversely affected by increased mortality from the Acquired Immune Deficiency Syn-drome (AIDS). This population level will also increase nearly ten-fold in the space of less than a hundred years. The rapid increase in the size of West Africa's population is buttressed by a fertility rate exceeding six children per woman, with every mother having, on average, more than three daughters as of the end of 1994. By the middle of the second decade of the twenty-first cen-tury, these daughters will, themselves, have become mothers.

Forty per cent of the inhabitants of the area lived in urban centres as of 1990 and the proportion is growing rapidly. Internal population movement and cross-border population flows are rife in the sub-region. Indeed, West Africans are reckoned to be amongst the most mobile people in Africa; they

4

are to be found in large numbers outside their countries and outside the region. One-third of the rural population of the sub-region does not live in the districts from which they originated. Similarly, 12% of the sub-region's population outside Nigeria does not live in their country of birth. Between 1960 and 1990, the urban population of West Africa grew five-fold; the ratio of urban residents increased from 14% in 1960 to 40% in 1990. By the year 2020, the ratio is expected to stand at 60%. Furthermore, there is a growing trend of migration southwards towards the coast, a fact which is already increasing population density in the area. In the major coastal settlements of the sub-region, the population density averages 124 inhabitants per sq km; by the mid-1990s, 41% of West Africa's population was already concentrated in the main coastal centres, which represent 8% of the land area.

On the basis of the above-mentioned demographic characteristics and trends, it seems clear that West African leaders and policy makers will have to brace themselves for major policy challenges. The first of these relates to just how the massive population that will live in the area in the next fifty years will be fed and provisioned. This has direct implications for agricultural development generally and a food security strategy in particular. Related to this is the capacity of West African governments and voluntary non-governmental organisations to provide the adequate infrastructural support essential to the pursuit of a decent livelihood. This question will be particularly relevant to the southerly, coastal population belts of the area where the majority of the inhabitants of the sub-region are increasingly concentrated. Further- more, given that the continuing intensity of internal and cross-border migration will result in the acceleration of the creation of multi-ethnic, multi-religious urban, semi-urban, and rural settlements, issues of the re-definition of citizenship rights will have to be re-visited. Presently, these rights are mostly closely tied to ancestral birth; this definition will certainly come under severe strain as more people live in settlements other than their places of origin or birth. The question of citizenship rights is likely to be just one of several political challenges that will flow from the demographic dynamics of the sub-region in the next few decades.

Ethno-Religious Pluralism

Without exception, all of the countries of the sub-region are ethnically plural; no ethnically homogenous countries like Botswana or Somalia exist in West Africa. In Nigeria alone, it is reckoned that there are some 250 ethnic groups many of which are divided into several sub-groups. Members of some ethnic groups are spread out across a number of countries in the sub-region. For example, the Yorubas are to be found in Nigeria, Benin, Ghana, and Côte d'Ivoire; Hausas in Nigeria, Ghana, and Niger; Kanuris in Nigeria, Niger, and Chad; the Wollofs in Senegal and the Gambia; Shuwa Arabs in Tchad, Nigeria, and Niger; Mandingos in Guinea, Guinea Bissau, Sierra Leone, and Liberia; Ewes in Ghana and Togo, Akans in Ghana and Côte d'Ivoire; Fulanis in virtually all the states in the region, and Tuaregs in Niger, Mali, and Burkina Faso. Furthermore, religious pluralism is the norm in most of the countries of the sub-region. The most commonly practised religions are Christianity (various versions), Islam (various versions) and a variety of 'traditional'/indigenous religions; syncretism is not uncommon. Although in some states, there is a preponderance of (nominal) Muslims over Christians and vice versa, all over West Africa, there are ethnic, religious and other minorities the management of whose affairs has direct implications for the conduct of governance and the prospects for national stability.

In the period from the late 1970s, especially following the Iranian revolution, there has been a revival of radical Islam in the West African sub-region. This revivalism has been particularly evident in the main urban centres and has resulted, in several countries, not only in inter-factional fights among Muslims of different sects but also clashes between Muslims and Christians and direct challenges to the secular nation-state project. At the same time, the growth of Christian Pentecostalism, mostly imported or inspired from America, has been in evidence and has also produced challenges to the secular constitution which most countries operate. Taken together with the revival of ethnic identities in all of the countries of the sub-region, it seems that religion and ethnicity will be key elements of the political terrain in West Africa, pushing the boundaries of the secular state to their limits. The worsening problem of economic decline in the area, as in the rest of Africa, and the heightening of social fragmentation as the quest for structural adjustment continues will probably keep the flame of ethnic and religious revivalism burning for a while. Already, in response to the diminution of the capacity of the state to meet its social responsibilities to the citizenry, religious and ethnic associations have been revived or established to play a role in social provisioning, and although this could be converted into a useful instrument in the renewal of civic culture, it could also result in the heightening of exclusivist forms of ethnic consciousness. Clearly, West African countries would need to reform their economies and political systems conscious of the need to better accommodate and benefit from their ethnic and religious plurality.

Inherited Languages in West Africa's Internal Geo-Politics

The countries of the sub-region are grouped together in the Economic Community of West African States (ECOWAS) which was founded in 1975 as a Togolese-Nigerian joint initiative. As we shall see later, each of the countries also belongs to a host of smaller organisations grouping a smaller number of states together. Although all of the countries of the sub-region signed the ECOWAS treaty and its protocols, there are several lines of division that continue to keep them apart and undermine their efforts at co-operation. Perhaps the most important of these is the one that corresponds to the lines of the colonial partition of Africa: four of the countries are Anglophone, being former colonies of Britain and members of the British Commonwealth; two, namely Guinea Bissau and Cape Verde, are Lusophone, being former Portuguese colonies; Liberia is English-speaking as it was founded with the help of the United States and has remained in the American sphere of influence; the remaining countries are Francophone, being former colonies of France and members of the French *Francophonie*. With English, French, and Portuguese being the lingua franca of the countries according to who their former colonisers were, the 'language divide' and the political load which it carries and symbolises has often been a factor militating against closer interaction among the countries of the sub-region. Matters are not helped by the massive influence which France continues to exert on its former colonies in West Africa, a point which will be addressed more fully later. The international geo-politics of the Francophone-Anglophone contest are all too often refracted into the West African sub-region with consequences on the will and scope for the extension of the boundaries of cross-cutting sub-regional co-operation.

If France's geo-political and commercial interests in Francophone West Africa have fed into the language divide and have, therefore, constrained the scope for fully-fledged regional co-operation across linguistic lines, a legitimate question to raise, and one which has generated debate and anxiety in Francophone West Africa, relates to the future of the 'special' links between Paris and its ex-colonies in the sub-region. This question has become all the more important in view of France's own commitment to the European Union. We will return more fully to this issue when we come to discuss the French factor in West Africa. Suffice it to note that the potential now exists in Francophone Africa for policy makers to begin to think of ways of forging ties with other countries/interests outside the *Francophonie* and it will certainly be a point of interest, both for policy and political reasons, to see how this potential 'flexibility' evolves in the next few years. Of course, it cannot be taken for granted that France's growing pre-occupation with the European Union will result in a complete disengagement from Francophone West Africa

— indeed, there is much talk in Paris of establishing a link between the CFA Franc and the Euro and France has played a pivotal role in encouraging greater co-ordination among the Francophone West African states within the Union Economique et Monetaire Ouest Africaine (UEMOA). It is, however, still possible that in the years ahead, as they cease to be 'special' to Paris, the Francophone countries will themselves seek to diversify their relations more aggressively and, in so doing, probably engage other West African states more intimately than is presently the case. Similarly, Nigeria, as West Africa's biggest economy, might also attempt to project itself much more fully both as a fallout from the resolution of its deep-seated problems of internal governance and as part of its own attempt at strengthening the ECOWAS framework for regional co-operation.

The Political Framework for Governance

A majority of the countries of the sub-region attained independence as multi-party systems, at least nominally. However, in many countries, multi-partyism soon gave way to single party or military rule. In those countries like Côte d'Ivoire and Senegal where the multi-party framework was maintained, one party, the party of the independence struggle, was over-whelmingly dominant. The rapidity with which military rule spread from Togo to encompass all the other countries of the sub-region, with the exception of Côte d'Ivoire and Senegal, and the rapid, often violent regime turnover that the region witnessed in the period up to the late 1990s, is symptomatic of the crisis of governance that continues to afflict the area. In the overwhelming majority of the countries in West Africa, political succession was, until the on-set of multi-party political reforms in Africa, unpredictable, achieved by un-constitutional means (mainly the coup d'état), and accompanied by violence. Even as most of Africa moved decisively during the late 1980s and early 1990s to embrace electoral pluralism, Nigeria, Sierra Leone, and the Gambia slid into military rule before massive local and international pressure compelled their military rulers to embrace programmes of transition to elected government. It is on account of the foregoing that many commentators consider West Africa to be one of Africa's most volatile regions. One test of the recent political re-forms which many of the countries of the sub-region have embraced, under local popular and donor pressure, will be their capacity to deliver orderly, constitutional succession on a sustained basis in the years ahead.

Most of the countries in the sub-region have convened and held multi-party elections as part of the political reform process that swept through much of Africa during the late 1980s onwards. As can be expected, all of the elections were bitterly contested and in the cases of Ghana, Guinea, and Côte d'Ivoire, sections of the opposition boycotted the polls altogether. In Senegal, violence associated with the contest between the incumbent regime and its opponents resulted in a number of key opposition leaders being arrested; in Togo, assassinations and attempted killings were rife and marred the entire electoral process. Only Mali, Benin, Cape Verde, and Niger had fairly open elections that were not too bitterly contested. It was also only in Cape Verde, Niger, Benin, and Mali that the electoral outcome resulted in the removal of incumbents from power. In Cape Verde, the incumbent government was beaten outright by the opposition; in Mali and Niger, the heads of the incumbent regimes that presided over the national conferences they had were not eligible contestants in the elections that took place; in Benin Republic, Mathieu Kérékou was already too weakened and discredited by the processes that led to the convening of that country's sovereign national conference to represent any serious source of challenge to the main opposition coalition. However, in the face of a gridlock between the president and parliament, Niger was to slide back to military rule before the late General Barre Mainasara transformed himself into an elected civilian president through an electoral process that was marked by fraud. The bitter aftermath of that process was to stalk Niger's political landscape until May 1999 when Mainasara was assassinated by his bodyguards and Niger was brought back to full military rule. In Benin, after a period in opposition, Kérékou was returned to power, adding to the number of West African countries — Ghana, Mali, Burkina Faso, etc. — where second elections, characterised by widely varying degrees of success, had been held as part of the renewed drive towards multi-party politics.

It seems clear from the evidence available on the elections that have been held in West Africa that the task of national reconciliation is still a major one in the sub-region and that the quest for democratisation is still fragile and may not necessarily deliver sustained political stability. The bitterness between the opposition and incumbents remains very strong in many countries. Matters have not been helped by the fact that across the sub-region, elected governments have had to stick to the implementation of unpopular International Monetary Fund (IMF)/ World Bank structural adjustment programmes which have fed into pre-existing economic difficulties to take a severe toll on the working and living conditions of the majority of the populace. Taken together with military rule in Niger, the number of elected governments headed by former military rulers, the absence of acceptable power-sharing mechanisms in hotly contested terrains like Côte d'Ivoire, Ghana, Burkina Faso, and, to a lesser extent, Senegal and Togo, the Tuareg rebellion in Mali, Niger, and Burkina Faso, the crisis in the Mano tri-state area, and the continuing tensions in the Casamance region, it would seem that a key theme that will dominate internal political debate in the years ahead will be the best electoral strategies and institutional approach for reconciling competing domestic political interests. Evolving a framework for reconciliation will not be easy given the numerous vested interests that have developed in support of competing claims for power. But it is clear that the evolution of such a framework will be indispensable to the quest for a return to the path of economic growth and development in West Africa.

One important feature of politics in West Africa, and one which is often not sufficiently remarked but which will be central to the future of the countries of the sub-region, centres around the mode of organisation of government in multi-ethnic, multi-religious societies. This is a question which is made all the more pressing by the fact that intra-state armed conflicts pitching various groups against one another, have increased in frequency in the sub-region. With the exception of Nigeria, all other West African states attained independence as Jacobin centralised state systems with the central government wielding a great deal of power. Nigeria was ushered into independence as a fairly loose federal system but the period since 1967, when the country's civil war started, has seen the rapid erosion of the basis of its federal system of government and the increased concentration of power in the central government. This is partly the result of prolonged military rule; for all but 10 years out of the 39 years since the country became independent in October 1960, the military has ruled Nigeria. Thus, all of West Africa was, in the period up to the 1990s, governed under highly centralised systems of government that were also, in most cases, underpinned by varying degrees of political authoritarianism.

The unitarist state project which the countries embraced was supposed to feed into their strategy for promoting national unity, integration, and economic development; the legitimacy crisis of the state created/exacerbated by the prolonged economic crisis in the region and the revival of ethnic and religious identities have posed direct challenges to the unitary, centralised state project. It would seem that the other dimension of the governance question in West Africa in the years ahead will centre on the most appropriate system of government necessary for the pursuit of the goals of national cohesion and rapid economic development: centralised/unitarist or decentra-lized/federalist/confederalist? This concern also touches directly on the choice between presidential and parliamentary systems and majoritarian and coalition-based governments underpinned by one type or the other of proportional representation. The increasing restlessness of minorities in Niger, Mali, Burkina Faso, (with their Touareg problem), Côte d'Ivoire (with the increasing friction between the so-called authoctons migrants, and Muslims in the north), Senegal (with its long-standing Casamance problem), Nigeria (with its deepening ethnic, religious and regional crises most sharply expressed in the oil-rich delta), Guinea (with the contest pitching Mandingos, Sousous, and Foullahs against one another), Ghana (Nanumbas vs Konkonbas, for example), and other countries suggests that the question of how best to administer the countries will remain a key issue in the years ahead.

Political Conflicts and Civil Wars

For all of the volatility and instability that have characterised politics in West Africa, it is amazing that, with the exception of Nigeria which slid into a civil war between 1967 and 1970 and discounting the on-off conflict in Senegal's Casamance province, the region knew no major systemic breakdowns until the very late 1980s/early 1990s when Liberia slid into a prolonged and devastating civil war. This war was to spread to Sierra Leone in 1993 with the consequence that the Mano tri-state area (which consists of the countries with an interest around the Mano River) became engulfed in war and disorder. Certainly, the crisis in the Mano tri-state area is the most serious systemic breakdown witnessed in the sub-region since the end of the Nigerian civil war. Liberia became the first country in West Africa to qualify for description as a 'collapsed' or 'failed' state on the same level as Somalia. In the Sahelian states of Mali, Burkina Faso, and Niger, the central governmental authorities were, from the late 1980s, locked in conflict with their Touareg populations, resulting in skirmishes between government troops and rebel fighters. The problems which some of the Sahelian states have with their Touareg populations are, however, far less serious than the Liberian and Sierra Leonean civil wars. Guinea-Bissau, too, was to slide into a civil war pitching rival sections of the army against each other. For the majority of the Francophone countries, a strong French presence, not just in terms of investments but also in terms of the siting of military posts and personnel, may have played a role in reducing the pressures towards separatism and internal civil war. Still, it is clear that for the foreseeable future, the promotion of reconciliation and reconstruction in war-torn societies and the prevention of systemic break down in the other countries will remain key features of politics and governance.

The project of reconciliation and reconstruction would, inevitably, involve close attention to the establishment of a new social contract between the state and society, the reconstruction of the state to redress the unidirectional retrenchment which it suffered during the adjustment years, and the provision of a new set of principles around which national energies could be mobilised and which could endow the state with a sense of purpose and coherence. Also, the issue of the type of economic policies which may best be attuned to the goal of national reconciliation and reconstruction would have to be addressed. Clearly, the trend whereby societies freshly emerging from conflict are made to adopt neo-liberal economic measures that are deflationary in thrust is one which would need to be re-thought and balanced against the need for the promotion of job-creating, infrastructure renewing and production-enhancing economic growth and development. Furthermore, the question of how to make the political system more repre- sentative of and responsive to the interests and concerns of the citizenry beyond periodic elections will need to be tackled. Finally, state capacity and legitimacy in curbing the traffic in light weapons that have flowed into West Africa in greater quantities than before and which have helped to fuel many an intra-state, inter-communual conflict will need to be addressed. As part of this process, a co-ordinated regional strategy might need to be considered for checking the activities of both international mercenaries and mercenary organisations as well as transnational mining interests engaged in illicit commercial trans- actions in the conflict zones of West Africa.

Boundaries that Unite or Boundaries that Divide?

The colonial partition of Africa, arbitrary and shoddy as it was, left most of the continent with 'artificial' boundaries that were bound to be sources of conflict. Members of some ethnic groups found themselves divided between two or three states while the life styles of nomadic groups like the Fulani and the Touareg were insufficiently catered for. In a bid to minimise the conflict potential, which the arbitrariness of the boundaries could generate, the Organisation of African Unity (OAU) decided that all inherited boundaries should be accepted and respected as demarcated by the forces of colonialism. It is, however, in West Africa that most of the (often violent) boundary disputes that have been witnessed on the continent have unfolded: Nigeria vs Cameroon; Nigeria vs Bénin; Nigeria vs Chad; Ghana vs Togo; Mali vs Burkina Faso; Burkina Faso vs Côte d'Ivoire; Senegal vs Mauritania; Guinea vs Sierra Leone etc. In several cases, the border disputes between neighbouring West African countries have degenerated into recurring, if often short-lived armed conflicts. These conflicts have often been fuelled by struggles over the control of human, mineral, or land resources.

Existing attempts at managing inter-state boundary disputes have mostly centred on the establishment of bilateral joint commissions or bilateral boundary commissions to map out areas of disagreement between the countries involved. These commissions have, however, not been successful at preventing the periodic outbreak of armed hostilities between neighbours in the sub-region. Beyond *ad hoc* mediation efforts put in place after border wars have started, there is no effective multilateral mechanism for preventing the outbreak of violent border disputes in the sub-region. The platform provided by ECOWAS has never been used for tackling boundary disputes; this is so in spite of the rhetoric in the late 1970s and early 1980s about an ECOWAS defence and security pact. Clearly then, boundary disputes will continue to constitute a significant element of the politico-security problems afflicting the sub-region in the years ahead, making the search for more creative approaches to managing borders for the mutual benefit of the countries a pressing policy and politico- diplomatic concern. At issue is the need to make efforts to ensure that borders unite rather than divide the peoples of West Africa both in *de facto* and *de jure* terms.

Coping with Desertification

With the exception of Mali, Burkina Faso, and Niger which are fully land-locked, the majority of the states of the sub-region consist of countries that have a coastal front on the Atlantic ocean, making them open to and accessible for international commercial interactions. It is common in recent literature on the sub-region to refer to the countries with an Atlantic flank as the coastal Sahelian states, an appellation which seeks simultaneously to underline the increasing desertification of the area as the Sahara encroaches southwards whilst acknowledging the existence of mangrove swamps and some belts of tropical rain forest in the southernmost parts of the coastal countries. The encroaching Sahara and the deterioration of agricultural land associated with the desertification process was a factor in the Sahelian droughts that were experienced in the area over the last 25 years, droughts which took their toll on livestock and human life and have resulted in a general downward movement of population towards the coast. The most well-known of the Sahelian droughts was the one that occurred in 1973 but in the period since then, there have been several others that, on the whole, have been no less devastating in their effects on the livelihoods of nomadic and desert groups in the northern zones of West Africa.

The problem of increasing desertification that has been a key element in the geo-ecology of West Africa provides an insight into a second dimension of the security problem in the sub-region, namely, food security. For, much of West Africa's food output comes from the savannah belt that is increasingly threatened by the desertification process; the sub-region's livestock population is also concentrated in the areas most threatened by the Sahara's encroachment. But beyond this, the desertification process points to a major aspect of the environmental crisis in West Africa. The southwards encroachment of the Sahara has a lot to do with the overgrazing of the savannah belt by livestock, the widespread practice of felling trees for wood fuel in rural West Africa, the pressure on farming land associated with non-intensive farming practices, and the varieties of erosion associated with them. Efforts at halting the desertification process through official tree planting campaigns have, on the whole, been ineffective. The multilateral effort represented by the Permanent Inter-State Committee for Drought Control in the Sahel (CILSS) which was set up with the assistance of the European Commission following the 1973 drought has also not been able to support a sufficient number and spread of projects that can stem the desertification process. Without doubt then, desertification will be one of the most important challenges which West African states will have to grapple with into the next century. As far as its food security implications are concerned, policy decisions would have to address the question of whether to strive for agricultural food self-sufficiency or, more controversially, to depend on the development of the capacity to import food from other regions of the world. Both options carry clear implications for policy direction and bear directly on the management of the economy.

Enduring environmental difficulties and the problem of food security are only two dimensions of the consequences that are likely to flow from the desertification process. A third dimension centres on the problems that are bound to result in the southerly flow of population in response to the encroaching desert. As we noted earlier, this process, already evident in the extremely rapid growth which coastal cities are experiencing, will not only strain existing physical and social infrastructure at a time of continuing economic crisis and structural adjustment-related austerity, it will also pose direct challenges to the widespread practice of tying citizenship rights to people's place of birth or origin, as opposed to their place of residence and site of labour. This has already arisen in Côte d'Ivoire, which has most immigrants of West African countries, and where the disqualification of Alassane Ouattara from eligibility to participate in the country's presidential elections on account of his alleged ancestry created restiveness among the long-term residents of the country originating from Burkina Faso, Ghana, Senegal and Mali. Yet, it is not at all certain, on present evidence, that there is a sufficient level of consciousness in the local polity and among the main donors active in West Africa, that remedial political measures need urgently to be introduced to address this problem in order to prevent future violent conflicts.

Shared Water Resources

The main internal waterways in the sub-region are the rivers Niger, Senegal, Mano, Volta, and Benue. Both the Niger and Senegal rivers are two of the seven most important bodies of water in all of Africa. From the overall regional point of view, by far the most important is the Niger which is also bigger than the Senegal. Emerging from the Futa Djallon mountains in Sierra Leone, it traverses several African countries before emptying itself into the Atlantic ocean through the Nigerian delta. In addition to its huge hydro-electrical potential, the Niger river is also home to a variety of marine life, especially fish, and a source of water both for household and industrial use and for farming activities. Given its strategic importance to the socio-economic development strategies of the countries of the sub-region, it is clear that it can be both a stimulant for tremendous levels of co-operation and a source of disputes between the countries that have an interest in the use to which it is put in the various countries it traverses during the course of its long journey from the mountains in Sierra Leone to the Atlantic delta of Nigeria. As the desertification process continues, the strategic significance of the Niger, Senegal, Volta, Mano, and Benue rivers to the water resource and agricultural development objectives of various West African states is bound to grow. So too will the potential for conflict.

It is perhaps a foretaste of the kinds of disputes which shared water resources have a potential for generating in West Africa that in the period since the 1960s, growing concerns have been expressed by interested countries about the use to which individual countries have sought to put the sections of regional rivers that traverse their territories. Nigeria, for example, had to address the concerns of some of its neighbours (especially Niger) when it embarked on the construction of the gigantic Kainji dam; it has also had cause to express its anxieties to Mali over attempts to tap from the Niger for rice irrigation and other agricultural purposes. Obviously, on the face of things at least, the easiest way to avert the possible outbreak of 'water wars' in the future will be to devise strategies for developing the full potentialities of the rivers in the wider framework of regional co-operation/integration in West Africa. This was attempted through the Mano River Union and the Organisation for the Development of the Niger River Basin; both agencies are, however, moribund as they were never really well-funded and were unable to attract sufficient international support for their operations. Thus, as it is, each country has basically been left to its devises as far as the use to which the shared rivers is put; the potential for conflict is open-ended.

In addition to the rivers that serve as a common resource for several of the countries of West Africa, the area also has two important lakes. These are Lake Volta and Lake Chad on the Northeast boundary of Nigeria with Chad. The former is listed among the biggest artificial lakes in the world and is a legacy of Nkrumah's grand vision for the agro-industrial transformation of Ghana. It is a source not only of water for domestic, agricultural and industrial use, but also of hydro-electric power for Ghana itself and its immediate neighbours like Mali, Burkina Faso, and Côte d'Ivoire. Fed by the Volta River, it is clear that any interference with the main source of water flow into the lake will have far-reaching consequences. Ghana has, therefore, always closely monitored the use to which the authorities in Burkina Faso put the section of the Volta River that traverses their territory. So far, open hostilities have been avoided in the management of the common interests which several West African countries have in the Volta River and Lake Volta, although in 1998, tension mounted between Ghana and Burkina Faso over the latter's decision to build a dam, which was blamed for the low water level at Akosombo and the disruption in electric power supply that Ghana suffered. Also, Nigeria and Chad have had occasion several times to exchange military fire over the use of Lake Chad, including the fishing rights of the boundary communities living near or around the lake. These hostilities have taken place in spite of the existence of a Nigeria-Chad Joint Commission that is supposed to harmonise the interests of both countries in the development and use of the resources of the lake. Interest in the lake and the territory around it has been heightened by suspicion that the area may be rich in hydrocarbons.

The Agrarian Base of Economies: Being Strengthened or Weakened?

The economies of the countries of the sub-region remain predominantly agri-cultural; most of the countries were ushered into independence as exporters of primary agricultural commodities like cocoa (mainly Nigeria, Ghana, and Côte d'Ivoire), coffee (principally Nigeria, Ghana, Côte d'Ivoire, and Sierra Leone), cotton (mainly Burkina Faso, Nigeria, Niger, Mali, Guinea, and Mau-ritania), palm produce (chiefly Nigeria, Sierra Leone, Liberia, and Côte d'Ivoire), rubber (mainly Liberia, Côte d'Ivoire, and Nigeria), and groundnuts (principally Senegal, the Gambia, and Nigeria). Livestock and hides and skin exports are also important to the economies of the region with the non-coastal Sahelian states dominating the trade. Furthermore, minerals like gold (Ghana), diamonds and rutile (Sierra Leone, Ghana and Guinea), columbite and tin (Nigeria and Guinea), uranium (Niger), crude oil (Nigeria), iron ore (Nigeria, Sierra Leone, and Liberia), limestone (Benin, Nigeria, and Sierra Le-one), and bauxite (Guinea and Sierra Leone) feature prominently in the export profile of the sub-region. In the years after independence, most of the countries of the sub-region, like the rest of Africa, witnessed a further narrowing of their export base as they increasingly depended on the export of one or two commodities for their revenues in their almost inexorable march towards monoculturalism. Countries like Nigeria and Sierra Leone took on a decisively rentier character as they depended almost exclusively on mineral rents for their revenues.

The bulk of the population of the sub-region, some 60%, remains rural and is immersed in agricultural activities. Because settler colonialism did not take root in the sub-region, the kinds of large-scale land alienation that were witnessed in parts of Eastern and Southern Africa did not occur in West Africa and the sub-region's agricultural output is overwhelmingly dependent on small-holder peasant households than on large-scale commercial farming. Plantation agriculture was, however, attempted in the sub-region, sinking its deepest roots in Côte d'Ivoire but also gaining ground in Nigeria, Ghana, and Senegal as corporate and non-corporate interests take to large-scale farming in the context of the continuing and prolonged economic crises in the area. Peasant agriculture has been accompanied by a lot of rural-rural and rural-urban migration; peri-urban farming, mostly on the outskirts of cities and towns, is also commonplace in the sub-region, sometimes tied to the livelihood strategies of urban workers and professionals to supplement their diminishing real wages and salaries with income generated from part-time farming in or near the main cities and towns. As in other parts of Africa, women are active members of the farming population of West Africa, participating in planting, harvesting, processing and marketing activities.

The rapid expansion of West Africa's population, coupled with the difficulties associated with raising peasant productivity, poses a major question with regard to the food security of the region. Against the background of declining agricultural output, which very quickly translated into a decline in the sub-region's share of international export markets, almost all the governments in West Africa attempted to improve agricultural output first through 'Green Revolution' programmes that amounted to little and then through market-led macro-economic reform efforts associated with International Monetary Fund (IMF)/World Bank-sponsored structural adjustment program- mes. Indeed, structural adjustment was initially legitimised as a pro- rural programme that allegedly aimed to shift the domestic terms of trade in favour of the farming populace and, in so doing, revive the agricultural fortunes of the countries of Africa. Thus, currency devaluation, trade liberalisation, and the commercialisation/privatisation/ liquidation of agricultural parastatals was undertaken as part of the effort to promote market-based incentives for the farming population. Yet, the programmes have, on the whole, not resulted in any dramatic increases in agricultural output or productivity, although increases, in absolute terms, may have been recorded for certain food and cash crops produced in the sub-region. The reasons for the lacklustre performance of the adjustment programmes have been extensively analysed in the literature and need not detain us here. Suffice it to note that key elements in the market reform programmes tended to cancel out one another with the consequence that they did not produce the envisaged results. The situation was not helped by the indiscriminate removal of input subsidies, the lack of attention to the infrastructure needs of the farming communities, the inadequacy of marketing and financing institutions, and the difficulties posed by the ever-diminishing international terms of trade for primary commodity exporters. The quest for an improvement in agricultural output and productivity, therefore, seems to be one area that will continue to attract a great deal of policy attention.

The Travails of Industry in West Africa

The countries of West Africa all attained independence with the hope that the promotion of rapid industrialisation would be an integral part of their quest for economic development. Without exception, they articulated policy measures aimed at promoting an import-substitution industrial strategy. Apart from the macro-economic policies which they followed, various governments also articulated a host of incentive measures aimed at attracting foreign investment in manufacturing and encouraging the participation of local capital in the process. Both where the local private sector was still weak and in the places where a sizable indigenous capitalist class had been created, the state took a direct part in the promotion of the industrial development process by entering into joint venture arrangements with multinational enterprises and local investors to undertake manufacturing production. The results which were recorded from this effort were mixed both at the national and sub-regional levels. Nigeria, Côte d'Ivoire, Ghana, and Senegal emerged easily as the four most industrially advanced countries in the West African sub-region measured by the size of their manufacturing sectors and the number of people employed in them. To varying degrees, all the countries of the sub-region were able to satisfy a portion of their consumer goods needs through local production. A growing cross-border trade in goods produced within the sub-region was also emerging.

However, although the 1960s and 1970s witnessed significant increases in the level of local manufacturing activity in West Africa generally and Nigeria and Côte d'Ivoire in particular, the sub-region's industrial development process was fraught with a lot of difficulties. For one, the entire import substitution strategy was dependent for its success on the continued capacity of the state to finance the import requirements of the manufacturing sector. These requirements included not only raw material inputs but also intermediate and capital goods. The implication was that any serious crisis in the capacity of the state to earn the foreign exchange with which to pay for the import needs of industry would immediately translate into a crisis for industry. This was all the more so as the manufacturing sector was mostly geared towards serving the domestic market; not being export-oriented, it contributed little to the balance of payments viability of the state, thereby becoming a source of pressure on available foreign exchange resources. Thus, when in the second half of the 1970s and in the early 1980s, West African countries experienced serious payments problems, many manufacturers were immediately affected, with some factories collapsing outright and others retrenching workers and scaling back their capacity utilisation levels.

At another level, manufacturing in West Africa in the period to 1980 was too heavily concentrated in the production of light consumer goods, with insufficient attention to intermediate and capital goods production. This imbalance in the manufacturing structure of West African countries was reinforced by the fact that on the whole, local value-added in the manufacturing sector was generally very low. Furthermore, there was very little internal linkage between agriculture and industry. These and other shortcomings ranked among the issues which the IMF/World Bank adjustment policies promised to redress; in fact, the market-based policies simply reinforced the crisis in the manufacturing sector, setting the countries of West Africa on the path to de-industrialisation. The devaluation of local currencies in Ghana and Nigeria significantly increased the cost of importation of inputs for use in industry; this experience was to be replicated in Francophone West Africa following the devaluation of the CFA Franc. Unable to meet the costs of importing their inputs, many factories simply resorted to further curbing their capacity utilisation levels and rationalising their workforce. This trend was further intensified by the adverse effects on local manufacturing of the implementation of trade liberalisation measures which resulted in the flooding of the regional market with cheaper imports, some of which were simply dumped. Also, the deregulation of interest rates resulted in astronomical borrowing costs which manufacturers were unable to cope with.

In the face of the difficulties facing manufacturers, there is a distinct possibility that West Africa risks being returned to a role simply as a producer of primary commodities and importer of consumer goods. This prospect is made all the more likely given that the new 'sunshine' industries that were supposed to emerge from the ashes of the collapsed import substitution factories have failed to materialise. The difficulty of undertaking local manufacturing in Africa under the conditions of structural adjustment has meant that not many new factories are being established in place of those that have collapsed or are collapsing. Yet, it is inconceivable that West Africa could ever hope to develop without industrialising. This is a challenge which the countries of the sub-region would need to address through the articulation of policies aimed at stemming the tide of de-industrialisation. Such policies would necessarily have to overcome the weaknesses of the earlier attempts at import-substitution industrialisation. They would also have to take account of the World Trade Organisation's tariff and other trade-related regimes, with a view to devising strategies for ensuring that their development needs are catered for. For, it is difficult to imagine that industrial development can occur on a sustained basis in Africa without some measure of state protection; similarly, opportunities that could be derived from the exploitation of regional economies of scale would have to be closely explored.

West Africa's External Debt Burden

The severe economic strains which West African countries have been under date back in some cases to the early 1970s when the Organisation of Petroleum Exporting Countries (OPEC) quadrupled oil prices and, in so doing, created severe balance of payments problems for most of the states of the sub-region. With the exception of Nigeria which is Africa's biggest oil exporter and also a member of the OPEC, all other West African countries were and still are net importers of oil. Combined with the diminishing terms of trade for their agricultural exports, their growing budgetary problems, and the inflationary consequences of their fiscal policies, the payments problems which the majority of West Africa states suffered as a result of the OPEC oil price increases of the 1970s translated into a domestic and external debt crisis in the early 1980s for the countries of the sub-region. As far as the external debt problems were concerned, these were mainly the result of the bilateral, multilateral, and private trade loans which the countries accumulated during the course of the 1970s but which they became increasingly unable to service by the early 1980s. Nigeria, which was a big winner from the OPEC oil price increases, was itself to join the bandwagon of economic crisis and external indebtedness following the collapse, in the early 1980s, of the world oil market.

Nigeria is, by far, West Africa's single biggest debtor nation; as of 1999, it owes some USD39 billion to members of the London and Paris Clubs as well as multilateral financial institutions like the World Bank. A majority of the countries however have debts that are about or over US$10 billion. Servicing the debt has been one of the greatest economic challenges facing West African countries. Burkina Faso's debt, for example, represents some 50 per cent of its Gross Domestic Product (GDP). For Togo, Senegal, Niger, Sierra Leone, Benin, Ghana, and Cape Verde, it is between 55% and 100% of their GDP. For Nigeria, Mali, Guinea, the Gambia, Côte d'Ivoire, and Mauritania, their external debt ranges between 110% and 200% of their GDP. Guinea Bissau's external debt is an astonishing 350% of its GDP. It is little wonder then that for much of the 1980s and 1990s, the entire sub-region suffered net resource transfers. With the exception of Nigeria and, to a lesser extent, Côte d'Ivoire, the debt of most West African countries is mostly owed to multilateral donors. Nine countries in the sub-region — Burkina Faso, Ghana, Mali, Mauritania, Guinea, Senegal, Benin, Guinea Bissau, and Sierra Leone owe 40% or more of their outstanding debts to the multilateral.

Given the massive levels of resources which the countries of the sub-region have had to devote to the servicing of their external debts, it is not surprising that during the 1980s, West Africa earned the dubious distinction of being home to some of the very poorest nations on earth. The human development surveys which the United Nations Development Programme (UNDP) carried out during the 1980s and early 1990s indicated clearly that Sierra Leone, the Gambia, Niger, Benin, Burkina Faso, Guinea Bissau, Guinea, Mali, and Liberia were among the most backward of the underdeveloped countries of the world. Nigeria was later to join the ranks of the poorest countries in spite of its vast human and mineral resources. Most of the countries of the sub-region are also categorised as having some of the harshest environments in the world for livelihood on account of the socio-economic, political, and environmental problems that are prevalent. None of the countries of the sub-region had a per capita GDP that was up to US$1,000 as of 1990; for 13 of them (Mali, Niger, Burkina Faso, Guinea Bissau, Guinea, Mauritania, the Gambia, Sierra Leone, Liberia, Togo, Bénin, Ghana, and Nigeria), it was under US$500. Similarly, the per capita income of the overwhelming majority of the countries was well below US$500 at the end of 1994. Some 45 per cent of the population of the sub-region live below the poverty datum level; the poor (including those in absolute poverty) will account for almost three quarters of the sub-region's total population. Amidst all of this, per capita aid was under US$100 for 12 out of the 17 countries that make up the sub-region.

Clearly, the magnitude of the debt problem in West Africa and the toll which it has taken on the social sector (especially health facilities and educational institutions) as well as on the sub-region's physical infrastructure is one which, if not contained, threatens to completely undermine the entire 'modernisation' process in the area. It is, in fact, partly in response to the decline of formal social institutions and the physical infrastructure that the process of informalisation has been accelerated (see discussion below). How to contain the debt crisis in West Africa beyond the traditional resort to rescheduling exercises and token gestures of cancellation (such as those that have been implemented within the ambit of the *Francophonie*, by the Group of Seven (G7) countries and the so-called Heavily Indebted Poor Countries (HIPC) Initiative will be one of the key economic policy challenges facing the sub-region and the donor community in the years ahead. It is now generally recognised that the prospects for economic recovery and a return to the path of growth will be enhanced by a substantial reduction in the debt service obligations of the debtor countries. This is likely to be the argument that will be pursued by West African leaders as there is neither appetite nor unanimity among them for the creation of a 'debtors' club that will enable them to push a collective case for debt repudiation.

France in West Africa: Does the CFA Franc Zone Have a Future?

France's central role in the West African sub-region has been a major focus of scholarly and policy debate for some time. It was the coloniser of nine out of the 16 countries that presently make up the sub-region. A key element of its colonial policy in Africa was the promotion of the 'assimilation' of the colo-nised into French culture through a systematic attempt at the denial and nega-tion of their indigenous cultures. Through the legacy of assimilation and a host of neo-colonial instruments and mechanisms, France's relations with its former colonies have remained very close in spite of the fact they became in-dependent in the early 1960s. Paris has a direct say in the internal political and economic affairs of the majority of the countries. Indeed, France maintains a military presence in several of them and has defence/security co-operation pacts with practically all of them. As members of the *Francophonie*, their alli-ance with France was and, to a great extent, still remains central to Paris' claim to a big power status in world affairs. French commercial interests span-ning practically all economic sectors not only dominate the economies of the Francophone countries but also enjoy privileged access to them through a combination of political, economic and cultural factors.

Perhaps the most important instrument through which France has developed its politico-economic grip on the Francophone countries is the CFA Franc. This is the common currency of all of the Francophone West African countries, with the exception of Guinea which had much earlier said 'Non' to Charles De Gaulle's neo-colonial project in Africa and opted for an autonomous path of its own, with its own national currency. Guinea maintained this course until Sékou Touré, its independence leader, died in office. The CFA was, from the outset, connected to the French Franc in a fixed parity. It was also convertible, with that convertibility guaranteed by the French Central Bank but fully backed by the foreign exchange earnings of the Francophone countries lodged with the Bank in Paris. Each of the Francophone countries maintained an account with the Bank of France and with the Banque Centrale des Etats de l'Afrique de l'Ouest (BCEAO) which serves as their common central bank. From 1948 to January 1994, the fixed parity remained unchanged at 50 FCFA to 1 FF. In January 1994, the parity was changed to 100 FCFA to 1 FF, a devaluation of 50%. That devaluation was preceded by the restriction of the convertibility of the CFA to its West African Francophone zone.

A lot has been written about the CFA Franc and its linkage to the French Franc. Much of the recent discussion has centred on the devaluation of the CFA Franc in January 1994. We would only note here that the arrangement whereby the currency was linked to the French Franc played an important part in bolstering the French currency as an international, freely convertible medium of exchange; but more than that, it conferred numerous advantages on French businesses by way of preferential access to the markets of the Francophone countries. For the leaders of the Francophone countries, in addition to the convertibility of their currency, which they seemed to cherish, the arrangement was perhaps the greatest symbol of the 'special' relations that they believed they enjoyed with France and its leaders. The devaluation of the CFA Franc was, therefore, an important matter laden with great symbolism for them. Did it, for example, mean the devaluation of France's relations with them? Beyond this, France's own increasing engagement with Germany and the wider European Union project has also raised questions about the future of the link between the French Franc and the CFA Franc. What does the abandonment of the Franc and the adoption by Paris and other key European players of a common currency mean for the CFA? Will the European Union be prepared to inherit France's commitments to the Francophone countries, including the guarantee of the convertibility of the CFA Franc? The questions are many and will increase as the European economic and political integration project gathers pace, however unevenly or unsteadily, in the years ahead. In a bid to re-assure local political and policy opinion across Francophone Africa, French officials have taken to suggesting that the relation between the CFA Franc and the French Franc will be transferred to the Euro. This has, however, fuelled a discussion on the appropriate rate of exchange at which the CFA Franc would be pegged to the Euro and the role which the new European Central Bank (ECB) might have in managing the hardness and convertibility of the CFA. Anxiety is widespread that a further devaluation of the CFA is perhaps inevitable.

Between Functional Regionalism and Regional Economic Integration

The West African sub-region is home to a large number of cross-national organisations that, nominally at least, are interested in the promotion of one aspect or the other of regional co-operation. Only one organisation, ECOWAS, exists with membership that cuts across the linguistic divide in the area. The existence of a large number of regional co-operation organisations is, by itself, not necessarily a bad thing. What is worrying for most observers, however, is the parallel mandate of many of the organisations which, in addition, are linguistically exclusive. In fact, several of these organisations compete with ECOWAS and duplicate its functions. Perhaps the most prominent of these is the Francophone Communauté économique des Etats de l'Afrique de l'Ouest (CEAO) which was set up soon after the founding of ECOWAS to perform broadly similar functions as ECOWAS in relation to the Francophone countries. The Union économique et monétaire Ouest africaine (UEMOA) formed in January 1994 as a successor to the CEAO also stands in direct competition with ECOWAS at a time when the latter's persistent funding difficulties continue unabated. West Africa is, therefore, suffused with regional co-operation and integration projects that do little co-ordination among themselves and whose record of achievement leaves much room for improvement.

Indeed, functional organisations which could carry out specific tasks, though numerous, have also been plagued with operational and financial difficulties. We have already cited the experience of CILSS and the problems it has encountered in carrying out its desert control tasks. The problems of the West African Clearing House (WACH) set up by the central banks of the sub-region are even worse; most countries simply do not use its services and, thus, its goal of promoting greater formal regional commercial and financial interaction has been frustrated. Several other examples can be cited of stalled, failed, or moribund efforts at functional co-operation. It would seem, therefore, that the sub-region is lost between functionalism and integration. Neither functionalism nor integration has been able to attract sufficient political/policy commitment (and finance) to make a significant difference in the levels of co-operation among the countries of the sub-region. The two are, of course, not necessarily incompatible; policy makers and donors will, however, have to decide which area to give greater priority in order to improve the livelihood chances of the majority of the people of the sub-region.

In the last three years, and with active support from France, the UEMOA has attempted to take a higher profile in the promotion of policy co-ordination among the Francophone countries of West Africa. These efforts have culminated in the creation of a common Francophone West African stock exchange based in Abidjan and poised to rival the existing stock exchanges in Nigeria and Ghana. Also, the Francophone countries are taking steps, within the framework of the treaty of the Organisation for the Harmonisation of African Business Law (OHADA), to streamline their commercial law in order, among other things, to enhance the smooth functioning of the Abidjan stock exchange. This is a significant development, even if there is plenty of room to doubt the efficacy of the promotion of stock market capitalism as one path towards Africa's quest for economic development. But perhaps equally interesting is the fact that the Francophone West African stock exchange is being promoted independent of the ones in Nigeria and Ghana where the authorities have also followed their own policy options without reference to a wider regional context. At the same time, ECOWAS is pursuing measures of its own aimed at increasing formal financial transactions within the sub-region, the most significant step in this direction being the launching of the ECOWAS traveller's cheque. Clearly, considerable scope for greater policy harmonisation and co-ordination exists and this ought to be exploited much more.

Sub-Regional Infrastructural Facilities

The development of infrastructural facilities in West Africa with a view to facilitating transport and communication in the sub-region has been one of the cardinal objectives of ECOWAS since its founding in 1975. In this regard, a great deal of emphasis was placed on the development of a trans-ECOWAS highway project from Lagos to Nouakchott and the promotion of a cross-border telecommunications system to ease contacts among the peoples of the sub-region. The record of achievement as far as the road project is concerned is highly uneven, with some sectors quite good and motorable all year round and others still undeveloped and only properly motorable during the dry season. The same is true for the telecommunications project where the goals achieved have been extremely modest. Although the days are gone when users of telephone services in Anglophone and Francophone Africa wishing to reach themselves had to go through exchanges in Paris and London, direct contact remains extremely tedious and is highly inefficient. Part of the reason for this is the slowness of the optic fibre telecommunication project approved by the leaders of the region to come on stream. Like the trans-ECOWAS highway, it has been stalled by severe financial difficulties. Both the highway and telecommunications projects are two areas where some donor support might be helpful; already, the African Development Bank has taken an active interest in the projects. Success in this area is central to any effort at promoting greater socio-economic and cultural interaction among the peoples of the sub-region.

Preparing West Africa for the Challenges of Globalisation

There is much consciousness across West Africa of the challenges of globalisation and the need to respond effectively to them to the benefit of the economies and peoples of the sub-region. Unfortunately, much of the scholarly and policy discourses are cast in terms of the need to avoid 'marginalisation' by increasing West African exports to the world market, attracting greater direct and portfolio foreign investment inflows, and promoting a generalised policy of market liberalisation, public enterprise privatisation, and capital account deregulation. In all of this, the accent is placed on the creation of a 'conducive' environment for private international capital to operate in the sub-region. But it is not at all certain that such an approach to responding to globalisation will necessarily launch West Africa on the path of sustained economic development which has been the object of policy-making since the defeat of colonial rule. Apart from the fact that no region of the world has ever developed on the basis of an unregulated market, there is a danger of focusing excessively on incentives that are geared towards the narrow interests of portfolio investors to the detriment of the kinds of long-term investment which the sub-region should be aiming to attract and for which a role for the state is indispensable. Furthermore, West Africa's capacity to respond to the forces of globalisation will be enhanced by a more systematic effort at promoting the investment activities of local entrepreneurs, especially those that enhance the sub-region's productive base in agriculture and industry. In part, this calls for a more concerted attempt at removing administrative and other barriers on intra-regional trade and investment in West Africa.

Sub-Regional Peace-Keeping

Following the onset of the Liberian civil war in the early 1990s, attempts were made to give teeth to the ECOWAS security and defence pact in order to stem the descent into anarchy in that country. The issue was, however, a highly divisive one since several countries, especially those supporting Charles Taylor, were suspicious of Nigeria's intentions given that it had initially openly supported the dictatorship of Samuel Doe. The Nigeria-led ECOWAS Monitoring Group (ECOMOG), which was eventually formed to serve as a peace-keeping force in Liberia was controversial from the outset, outrightly opposed by Côte d'Ivoire, Burkina Faso and several other Francophone countries. This fact, and the indiscipline of the ECOMOG force, contributed a great deal to the prolongation of the intervention and raised questions about the efficacy of the initiative. However, hailed as a major initiative at regional peace-keeping and conflict resolution at a time when the leading powers were unwilling to commit troops and resources to peace-keeping in Africa, and in spite of the numerous difficulties which it encountered — military, politico-diplomatic, and financial — ECOMOG was to have its mandate extended to Sierra Leone where, with Nigerian troops at its core, it helped to restore the elected civilian government of Ahmad Tejan Kabbah that had been toppled by a combined RUF/renegade Armed Forces of Sierra Leone fighters. Following the outbreak of fighting in Guinea-Bissau, ECOMOG was also to establish a presence there in a bid to restore some order ahead of fresh elections. But before the elections could be held, one of the main antagonists succeeded in overrunning the other, resulting in the fall from power of President Vieira.

Organising West African Women for Development and Equality

Most West African communities are heavily patriarchal in orientation. Even in 'matrilineal' Ghana, women are generally subordinated to men and bear a disproportionate part of the burden for reproducing society. In a bid to strengthen the prospects for greater equality for women in the development process, various women's organisations from Anglophone and Francophone West Africa came together to found the West African Women's Association (AFAO-WAWA) as the latest in a series of efforts at organising women in the sub-region for the collective promotion and defence of their interests. Its work is an admixture of advocacy, awareness-building, and project support (especially of the income-generating type relevant to women). It encourages all women's associations at the national and domestic level to work with it and, in this respect, is basically aiming to be an umbrella organisation. Its success will depend on its ability to establish itself as a credible body worth supporting by West African women and interested donors. Certainly, its interest in promoting women's income-generating activities fits in well with numerous projects promoted by local groups and NGOs in various countries aimed at achieving the same objective.

The Widening Frontiers of Informalisation

Perhaps more than other parts of sub-Saharan Africa, West Africa is an area where informal economic activities are most widespread. These activities span virtually all economic sectors and cover both domestic retailing and cross-border trading activities. Informal sector operations are evident in the financial sector through the activities of parallel market currency dealers, local-level money lenders, and community-based savings clubs; informal production structures mostly take the form of cottage-type manufacturing. But it is in the commercial sector, and the financial processes associated with it, that informal sector structures and processes have been most fully developed. Women play a very prominent role in informal commercial operations not just as retailers at the domestic level but also in the transborder transactions that have been booming over the years. Indeed, so central are women to West Africa's informal trade that many myths have been developed about the ubiquitous West African 'market mammies' and the vast resources which they control. Yet, not all of the women have managed to transform their informal sector activities into sites of accumulation; a majority remain at the level of subsistence in a market characterised by very intense competition and serving low income households. As of the end of 1990, it is reckoned that about 40% of the entire population of West Africa was involved in informal sector activities of one kind or another.

Much of the inter-state trade in West Africa is accounted for by the informal sector. Indeed, while formal commercial exchanges between the countries of the area amount to just over 5% of their total exports, informal sector flows are way more significant and are increasing. Small-scale traders shift resources from places as far apart as Nigeria and Senegal in West Africa and Nigeria and Niger in Central Africa in their search for markets; they were aided in this by the free convertibility of the Francophone CFA Franc. The suspension in August, 1993 of the CFA Franc's convertibility outside of the West and Central African zones did not however deter the informal sector operatives. Most observers/commentators seem to share the view that informal sector commercial flows are destined to inherit a greater share of sub-regional trade in spite (perhaps even because) of the many obstacles that stand in the way of formal trade flows. This way, it is expected that the economies of the countries of the sub-region will get increasingly integrated even if formal regional co-operation efforts such as those represented by ECOWAS continue to be plagued by problems or come to grief.

The commodities which are traded by the informal sector operatives across boundaries consist of imports brought in from Europe, North America, and the Far East into one or more of the countries in the area and then re-exported to other parts of the sub-region. Bénin Republic is, by far, one of the most important re-export centres in West Africa although Niger and Senegal are also significant players in this regard. The former colonial powers in West Africa, especially Britain and France, remain the main trading partners of the countries of the sub-region; they are also the leading sources of foreign investment in the area. However, commodities produced by locally established factories in various West African countries are also widely circulated by the informal sector operatives. One key issue which has, however arisen during the adjustment, is the impact of the manufactured goods that are informally traded in the sub-region on local industrial production in a context where a growing proportion of such goods consist of cheap imports from the Far East. From a policy point of view, there is concern that the widening disconnection between the goods that are traded informally and the local manufacturing structures in the sub-region is feeding into the dynamics of de-industrialisation. It is doubtful that regional integration could ever be sustained in the long-term if the local structures of production are being undermined by the patterns of informal commerce that are taking place.

Civil Society

One final issue that we would like to raise here relates to the nature of civil society in West Africa. At one level, given the early entry of the region into anti-colonial nationalism and radical as well as moderate forms of Pan-Africanism, several West African countries were home to a host of civil society associations, including youth organisations like the West African Students Union (WASU), which served as platforms, in the post-1945 period, for agitation for an end to colonial rule. The rapid spread of Western education in the region acted as a catalyst in the formation and proliferation of civil society organisations like the professional associations of lawyers, doctors, journalists, and teachers. The development of the colonial economy itself spawned a number of local interest groups associated with the emergence and spread of capitalist relations. Perhaps the most prominent of them were the trade unions of workers, the associations of farmers set up to promote their case for better prices, and the chambers of commerce that brought various categories of business people together. Added to these are the innumerable town/community development associations/unions for which West Africa, especially its Anglophone component is famed. These associations/unions, though set up to serve a developmental purpose fed into the process of the 'thickening' of West African civil society as did the establishment, by the 'educated elite'/les assimilés, of independent newspapers.

West Africa's Future Prospects: The Pessimists Versus the Optimists

In seeking to come to terms with the West African scene in all of its complexity and variety, scholars engaged in overview analyses of a retrospective/prospective kind have tended to fall into two broad categories. The first category, typified by the work of Robert Kaplan entitled 'The Coming Anarchy' and published in 1994 in the *Atlantic Monthly*, is an extremely pessimistic one which sees only an Armageddon awaiting the countries and peoples of West Africa on account of trends in the political economy of the sub-region. According to Kaplan, prolonged economic crisis, widespread social fragmentation, including the widening of the gulf between the rich and the poor, collapsing public institutions, worsening problems of corruption and lack of public accountability, increasingly illegitimate states, and rising ethnic, regionalist, and religious identities, especially Islamic religious identities, have combined to pose direct threats to political order and stability in the sub-region. The absence of any mitigating factor suggests that the area is headed for a major anarchy which can only be prevented through some form of external intervention. Already, several parts of the West African sub-region are enmeshed in civil conflicts; those places where systematic breakdown has not occurred are time bombs waiting to explode. Cronyism, drug peddling, prostitution, urban squalor, gangsterism, widespread and worsening poverty, and a range of illicit transactions have eaten deep into the fabric of society and refracted themselves into public institutions as to render them completely ineffective.

According to Kaplan (1994), the West African sub-region is witnessing:

> The withering away of central governments, the rise of tribal and regional domains, the unchecked spread of disease, and the growing pervasiveness of war.
>
> ...
>
> West Africa is reverting to the Africa of the Victorian atlas. It consists now of a series of coastal trading posts, such as Freetown and Conakry, and an interior that, owing to violence and volatility, is again becoming as Graham Greene once observed, 'blank' and 'unexplored'.

In direct and complete contrast to the extreme pessimism of the school represented by Kaplan is the strong optimism projected by the studies undertaken under the direction of Jean-Marie Cour and Brah Mahamane for the Club du Sahel. Anchored on the assumption that the rapid growth and re-distribution of population is West Africa's most restrictive yet dynamic characteristic, Cour, Mahamane and their colleagues attempted to show, through retrospective and prospective analyses, how the mobility of West Africa's 'energetic' population has brought about massive structural changes in the economy and society, including settlement patterns. The capacity of the peoples of the sub-region to quickly adapt themselves to changing circumstances and, in so doing, to improvise and innovate has been central to their efforts at improving their livelihood chances. As they point out, 'In a situation of rapid population growth, West Africans have striven with great vigour and individualism to improve their living conditions'. As a consequence of the high mobility of the population of the sub-region, mobility which includes cross-border flows of peoples, the pace of urbanisation and of the economic processes, industrial and agricultural, associated with it have accelerated. In the towns to which most migrants settle, 'citizens have invested savings and labour to make their surroundings acceptable'. Furthermore, '...they have created jobs to absorb the uninterrupted influx of migrants. ...Farmers, for their part, have moved closer to population centres where their products find more reliable outlets than in areas of more scattered settlement'.

Cour, Mahamane and their collaborators note that for the foreseeable future, there can be no doubt that exceptional levels of population growth and exposure to the world market will continue to exert a direct influence on the countries of the sub-region. These twin factors will further the trend of southward shift of West Africa's population towards the coast, accelerate the market orientation of farming and, in so doing, ensure some degree of food security, improve the capacity of the peoples to meet their requirements for goods and services, and make social and economic competition the norm in the sub-region. All together, West Africa is poised for massive structural change and the outlook, from a demo-economic perspective, is not one that gives cause for negative concern given the record of flexibility and adaptability of the peoples of the area. The international community can assist this process of structural transformation by making available long-term financing in the context of a long-term partnership and a sharp reduction in the level of donor involvement in the definition of national policy objectives. As to the countries of West Africa themselves, they would do well to maintain and even extend their policy of free movement of people within the broader framework of sub-regional co-operation as this will be beneficial to their quest for economic development, especially with regard to the expansion of regional markets.

Alternative Futures for West Africa in the Next Millennium

The projections for West Africa produced by the two dominant schools in the on-going discourse about the future of the sub-region raise a lot of questions.

Kaplan's analysis has been severely criticised as much for what some commentators see as its underlying racist undertone as for its thinly disguised invitation for the re-colonisation of the sub-region. We would add that his extreme pessimism assumes that events can only follow one downward course as if there are no actors or actresses within (and outside) the sub-region with an objective and subjective interest in reversing the trend of economic decline and social fragmentation and, in so doing, turning the table of underdevelopment and authoritarian governance. As to the works of Cour, Mahamane and their colleagues, the main weakness of their optimistic projection is that it is overwhelmingly based on a one-sided confidence on the positive outcomes that will be associated with rapid population growth and migration and exposure to the world market. Surely, an incapacity to adequately manage the socio-economic and political stimuli that population growth and flows might trigger cannot be ruled out of any scenario that is anchored on demography. But it is precisely this that Cour and his colleagues do.

So what future awaits West Africa in the years ahead? On the whole, it would seem that the options before the countries of the sub-region will centre around a straight choice between a greater effort at promoting regional co-operation or persisting with individual national efforts with little or no cross-country co-ordination. Most West African policy makers are aware of the similarity of the problems that confront their countries; they are equally aware that they have to take dialogue with one another more seriously. Yet, the impediments that stand in their way are many, not least among them the French factor and Nigeria's lingering crisis of governance as well as the political difficulties in several other West African countries. On the evidence that is available presently though, it seems likely that most countries will continue to try to develop individual national strategies whist paying comparatively smaller attention to regional integration. Perhaps the best that can be hoped for is that the governments will be inclined to integrate some regional perspective into their national strategies. Most of the governments themselves will have more than their fair share of internal political problems to worry about in the years ahead and since politics dictates a lot of what happens in the area, it can be expected that a great deal of policy attention and political energy will be devoted to managing domestic affairs. Unfortunately, popular, civil-society pressures for concerted regional co-operation remain underdeveloped in West Africa; the continuing economic crisis in the area will also limit the scope for functional forms of co-operation. The expansion of cross-border informal sector exchanges will, however, ensure that the boundaries of interaction among the peoples of the sub-region are widened.

In sum, it would seem that the future of the sub-region will lie somewhere in between the extreme pessimism of Kaplan and the wild optimism of Cour and his associates. Several factors, including the performance of the economy, the quality of governance, the capacity of civil society to organise and assert itself, the outcome of Nigeria's deepening crisis of governance, and the long-term global strategy of France, could act to sway the balance more in one direction rather than the other. The remarkable adaptability and innovativeness of the people in difficult circumstances, including their capacity to devise multiple livelihood strategies and popular alternative forms of provisioning should, however, mean that many will manage to live at or just above subsistence in spite of all indicators that point to a continuing crisis in the formal economy. It is such resilience and adaptability that explain why the sub-region has not previously been engulfed in widespread, all-encompassing anarchy and although these attributes should not be taken for granted, they probably will still ensure that the countries somehow manage to keep ticking on. Such is the centrality of West Africa's human resources to its survival and future prospects. The creative harnessing of these resources should help ultimately to rid the area of underdevelopment. Perhaps it is to the harnessing of these human resources on a sub-regional scale that political and policy attention need to be focused much more. For, it is in successful regionalism that West Africa's full potentials are likely to be realised both at the national and sub-regional levels.

Bibliography

Ate B. and Akinterinwa B., 1992, *Nigeria and its Immediate Neighbours*, Lagos, NIIA.

Bach Daniel et al (eds), 1988, *Le Nigeria: Un pouvoir en puissance*, Paris, Karthala.

Bossard Laurent, 1994, *Nigeria and the Perspectives for Regional Integration in West Africa*, Paris, Club du Sahel/CINERGIE.

CILSS/Club du Sahel/CINERGIE, 1995, *Preparing for the Future: A Vision of West Africa in the Year 2020*, Paris, CILSS/Club du Sahel/CINERGIE.

CINERGIE, 1993, *Regional Economic Integration Issues Between Nigeria, Benin, Cameroun, Niger and Chad*, Cotonou Meeting May 6-8, 1993, Mimeograph.

Egg J. and Igué J., 1993, *L'Integration par les marchés dans le sous-espace 'Est': L'Impact du Nigeria sur ses voisins immédiats*, INRA/UNB/IRAM, Club du Sahel, CILSS; also published in English as *Market-Driven Integration in the Eastern Sub-Market: Nigeria's Impact on its Immediate Neighbours*.

Ezenwa U., 1992, *Assessment of the Impact of Selected Economic Integration Instruments: Sectoral Transformation and Restructuring in West Africa*, Addis Ababa, ECA.

Gibbon P., et al, 1993, *A Blighted Harvest: The World Bank and African Agriculture in the 1980s*, New Jersey, Africa World Press.

Ibrahim J., 1995, *West Africa and the Federal Question: Nigeria's Bad Example*, Zaria, Mimeo.

Igué J. and Soulé B., 1992, *L'Etat entrepôt au Bénin: Commerce informel ou solution à la crise*, Paris, Karthala.

Kaplan R., 1994, 'The Coming Anarchy', *Atlantic Monthly*, February.

Lavergne R. (ed.), 1997, *Regional Integration and Co-operation in West Africa: A Multidimensional Perspective*, New Jersey, Africa World Press.

Mahamane B. et. al., 1993, *Regional Co-operation and Integration in West Africa* , Paris and Abidjan, OECD/CINERGIE/ADB.

M'bunyinga E., 1982, *Pan-Africanism or Neo-Colonialism?*, London, Zed Books.

Nwokedi E., 1985, 'Strands and Strains of Good Neighbourliness: The Case of Nigeria and its Francophone Neighbours', *Genève-Afrique*, Vol. XXIII, no. 1.

Obiozor G., Olukoshi A. and Obi C. (eds.), 1994, *West African Regional Economic Integration: Nigerian Policy Perspectives for the 1990s*, Lagos, NIIA.

Olukoshi A. et al, 1994, *Structural Adjustment in West Africa*, Lagos, Pmark/NIIA.

Olukoshi A., 1995a, 'The CFAF Devaluation Revisited', SAPEM, Vol. 8, no. 7.

Olukoshi A., 1995b, 'Understanding the Basis for the Reversal of Nigeria's Economic Policy Direction', SAPEM, Vol. 8.

Osterdahl I., 1997, *La France dans l'Afrique de l'après Guerre froide: Interventions et justifications*, Document de Recherche 2, NAI Uppsala.

Soderbaum F., 1996, *Handbook of Regional Organizations in Africa*, NAI, Uppsala.

Ubogu R.E., Ubogu and Orimolade W.A., (eds.), 1984, *Trade and Development in ECOWAS*, New Delhi, Vikas Publishing House.

Vogt M.A. (ed.), 1992, *The Liberian Crisis and ECOMOG: A Bold Attempt at Regional Peace Keeping*, Lagos, Gabumo.